...y holding a pen
...moves. I hope I become
human soon.

Two summers ago, I was invited as a guest to an anime convention called Anime Expo. I wasn't too thrilled about it at first, but the people who I went with were so funny that I found myself laughing for 10 days straight. It turned out to be a very valuable experience. I've tried to keep the enjoyment of "laughter" in mind while drawing this series. It might be hard to make you laugh out loud, but it would make me really happy if I could at least make you chuckle.

—**Nobuhiro Watsuki**

Nobuhiro Watsuki earned international accolades for his first major manga series, **Rurouni Kenshin**, about a wandering swordsman in Meiji Era Japan. Serialized in Japan's WEEKLY SHONEN JUMP from 1994 to 1999, **Rurouni Kenshin** quickly became a worldwide sensation, inspiring a spin-off short story ("Yahiko no Sakabatô"), an animated TV show and a series of novels. Watsuki's latest hit, **Buso Renkin**, began publication in WEEKLY SHONEN JUMP in June 2003.

BUSO RENKIN
VOL. 1
The SHONEN JUMP ADVANCED
Manga Edition

STORY AND ART BY
NOBUHIRO WATSUKI

Translation and English Adaptation/Mayumi Kobayashi
Touch-up Art & Lettering/James Gaubatz
Design/Yukiko Whitley
Editor/Michelle Pangilinan & Urian Brown

Managing Editor/Frances E. Wall
Editorial Director/Elizabeth Kawasaki
VP & Editor in Chief/Yumi Hoashi
Sr. Director of Acquisitions/Rika Inouye
Sr. VP of Marketing/Liza Coppola
Exec. VP of Sales & Marketing/John Easum
Publisher/Hyoe Narita

Printed in the U.S.A.

Published by VIZ Media, LLC
P.O. Box 77010
San Francisco, CA 94107

SHONEN JUMP ADVANCED Manga Edition
10 9 8 7 6 5 4 3 2 1
First printing, August 2006

www.viz.com

THE WORLD'S
MOST POPULAR MANGA
SHONEN JUMP
ADVANCED
www.shonenjump.com

SHONEN JUMP ADVANCED MANGA EDITION

Buso Renkin
ブソウレンキン

Vol. 1
New Life

STORY & ART BY
NOBUHIRO WATSUKI

BUSO RENKIN
Volume 1: New Life

CONTENTS

CHAPTER 1: NEW LIFE
Nobuhiro Watsuki

16

IT'S THE BELL.

GO! OR DO YOU WANT MORE DEMERITS?

EH?!

RING

YOU'RE NOT ALLOWED TO LEAVE UNTIL YOU'RE DONE.

I DON'T CARE IF IT TAKES YOU ALL NIGHT.

... YOU ...

FOUND ...

RUSTLE RUSTLE

DON'T YOU THINK MITA'S BEEN ACTING STRANGE LATELY?

LUNCHTIME

WHAT DO YOU THINK?

YOU THINK? I'VE ALWAYS THOUGHT HE WAS THE HARDEST TEACHER TO DEAL WITH AT SCHOOL.

RUSTLE RUSTLE

HEY MAHIRO!

AH!

FOUND YOU GUYS!

I SEE. YEAH, HE'S NOT GOOD AT ROCK-PAPER-SCISSORS.

TAK TAK TAK

HUH? WHERE'S MY BROTHER?

HE WENT TO BUY US DRINKS.

GOT 'EM!

REALLY?

THE UNIFORM LOOKS GOOD ON YOU.

CONGRAT-ULATIONS ON GETTING INTO OUR SCHOOL.

THANKS.

TO BE HONEST, I WANTED TO COME TO THIS SCHOOL

...BECAUSE I LOVED THE UNIFORM SO MUCH!

I'M GLAD TO HEAR THAT.

WHAT?

YOU TOO?

NO POINT IN HIDING IT NOW! I WANTED TO GO TO THIS SCHOOL BECAUSE I LOVED THE UNIFORM TOO!

ME TOO.

BLUSH

HMM?

YOU'RE IN A GOOD MOOD, MAHIRO.

22

GREEN VEGETABLE JUICE DX

Takamushi

Even Veggie Bug recommends it!

素+110%

500ml

WITH FISH MINT

HERE. I'LL GIVE YOU MINE. DRINK IT.

EH? ARE YOU SURE?

IT'S A PRESENT TO MY DEAR LITTLE SISTER FOR GETTING INTO OUR SCHOOL.

AH.

NEW MESSAGE

MAYBE I SHOULD HAVE KNOWN YOU'RE HEALTHY AS CAN BE?

SLURP SLURP

OHHH!

SHE'S DRINKING IT!

THEY'RE DEFINITELY SIBLINGS!

I CAME BECAUSE I WAS WORRIED ABOUT THIS MORNING, BUT...

I'M GLAD YOU'RE DOING WELL.

YOU'RE ALWAYS ...

...DOING SOMETHING RECKLESS.

ACTUALLY, NOT REALLY.

MY HEART IS STILL HURTING A LITTLE BIT.

THINK ABOUT IT, WILL YA!

I HADN'T THOUGHT ABOUT THAT.

HMM...

YEAH. YOU'RE LUCKY YOU SURVIVED THIS MORNING.

WHAT IF YOU REALLY GOT HURT?

YOU THINK?

AS LONG AS MAHIRO'S OKAY, I CAN TAKE A FEW BRUISES.

WELL...

MY BODY MOVES FASTER THAN MY BRAIN, SO IT'S BEYOND MY CONTROL.

I NEVER WANT TO BE AFRAID AND IN PAIN!

HECK NO!

KEEP IT UP, AND YOU'RE GOING TO DIE LIKE YOU DID IN YOUR DREAM LAST NIGHT.

SHOCK

RING...

OH NO!

I HAVE PHYS-ED NEXT!

AHH!

IT'S THE BELL.

24

26

HEY, WHERE ARE YOU GOING?

I SHOULD PROBABLY HELP HIM...

ALSO...

...IF HE'S NOT DONE WITH HIS PUNISHMENT.

WHAT A GOOD SISTER.

OH... I'M GOING TO FETCH MY BROTHER.

HE'S PROBABLY SHAKING AND TREMBLING IN FEAR RIGHT ABOUT NOW.

TUP

HUH?

WELL, IT DOESN'T MATTER EITHER WAY.

ARE YOU DONE...

...PULLING THE WEEDS...?

SHUP

35

I'M GOING TO TRY TO OUT-RUN IT!

IT'S NO USE.

...I SEE.

YOU HAVEN'T REMEMBERED EVERYTHING YET.

THEY'LL FOLLOW YOU TO THE ENDS OF THE EARTH AND THEY WILL KILL YOU.

THEY WON'T ALLOW ANY WITNESSES.

TO KEEP THEIR EXISTENCE A SECRET...

ONCE INVOLVED...

THERE'S NO PLACE TO RUN.

48

Kazuki Muto

- Height: 170 cm; Weight: 59kg
- Born: December 1st; Sagittarius; Blood type: O; 16 years old
- Favorites: Curry rice, green veggie juice, golden yellow color, older women
- Dislikes: Shitake mushrooms, math
- Hobby: Reading manga
- Things he is good at: A lot of things ("No point in hiding it now! I'm a Master of XYZ!")
- Affiliation: Private Ginsei Academy 2nd Year High School Student (Classroom B) E Dorm resident

Author's Notes

- He is a character who will grow and be liked by people. It was difficult to draw him while thinking of him as the main character. Instead I decided to go back and use all the characters I enjoyed drawing as his base.
- For some reason Misao Harumachi from *Rurouni Kenshin* stood out. I conceptualized Kazuki by imaging Misao as a male high school student in the present. (You can still see some resemblance in his bangs.)
- The reason he's a bit of a space cadet is because I was thinking about mainstream characters from various recent Shonen manga. I also figured, that between a space cadet and a joker, people would prefer the space cadet more.
- He doesn't like pain and being scared, but he can act tough in order to protect others. This character makes me feel like I want to draw the progression of how he grows stronger and becomes more caring while at times feeling hesitant.

"NONE OF THESE SUCCEEDED BUT ALCHEMY BECAME ONE OF THE PRECURSORS AND THE BASIS...

OF RECENT AND MODERN SCIENCES."

BLUSH

I WAS BORN LIKE THIS!

IT... IT'S NOTHING!

WHAT'S WRONG? YOU'RE MAKING A STRANGE FACE.

?

I SEE... MUST BE TOUGH.

POSE!

YOU JUST SAID, NONE OF IT SUCCEEDED.

SHKK

WAIT A SEC.

HUH?

IT WAS A SUCCESS OF SUPER-PARANORMAL PROPORTIONS. IT WAS UNEXPLAINABLE BY THE NORM. THEY ARE...

ONLY TWO TYPES OF ALCHEMY SUCCEEDED.

WHAT THEY SAY HERE IS "PUBLIC KNOWLEDGE."

FWAP

SSS!...

THE HOMUNCULUS WAS THE RESULT OF STUDIES ON ARTIFICIAL LIFE.

THE BUSO RENKIN CAME FROM WEAPONRY DEVELOPMENT.

BUT BOTH PROVED TO BE TOO DANGEROUS.

TOK   TOK

THEY'RE DANGEROUS!

YEAH.

SHH

AS A RESULT, IT WAS SWORN TO SECRECY.

I THOUGHT I WAS GOING TO DIE.

I WAS SCARED...

I WAS IN PAIN...

ONLY THOSE WHO PRACTICED ALCHEMY WOULD KNOW ABOUT IT.

TREMBLE TREMBLE

SHAKE

SHAKE

GRAB

BUT...

62

68

THANKS.

FSW

IT'S BECAUSE YOU'RE NOT WEARING YOUR SWEATER. HERE.

SHIVER

AA!

IT'S REALLY COLD!

I SEE.

I FELL IN THE SCHOOLYARD AND HIT MY HEAD...

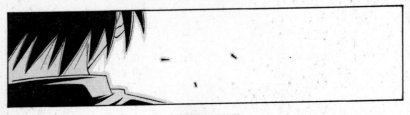

HMM... I SEE.

THAT'S A RANDOM QUESTION.

I'M 161CM.

HEY MAHIRO, HOW TALL ARE YOU NOW?

SHE WAS SO SMALL...

HER SHOULDERS ...

SQUEEZE

SHA

THAT LONG?

NO WONDER IT'S SO COLD.

ABOUT HALF AN HOUR.

PSH

LOCK

FWWWW

AH! WHAT THE...!

THE WINDOW'S OPEN. HOW LONG HAS IT BEEN OPEN?

COME ON. LET'S GO HOME!

THAT SHOULD DO IT.

74

CLASP

ALCHEMIST WARRIOR!

IT'S NOT EASY WORKING ALONE!

GHH

TSK!

IT WAS HIDING AMONGST THE CARCASSES!

I GOT HER, SARU-WATARI!

ZZ

WA

I'M HOME!

YEAH, I ASKED HIM THAT TOO.

HE WAS WITH ME UNTIL THE ENTRANCE. HE TOLD ME HE HAD ANOTHER ERRAND TO RUN SO HE WENT OUT AGAIN.

THIS LATE?

IT COULDN'T WAIT UNTIL TOMOR-ROW?

BUT HE SAID...

HAA HAA WELCOME HOME MAHIRO.

HAAA

HAAA

Damn it!

HUH? WHERE'S KAZUKI?

BLERP

Damn it!

BLEEP

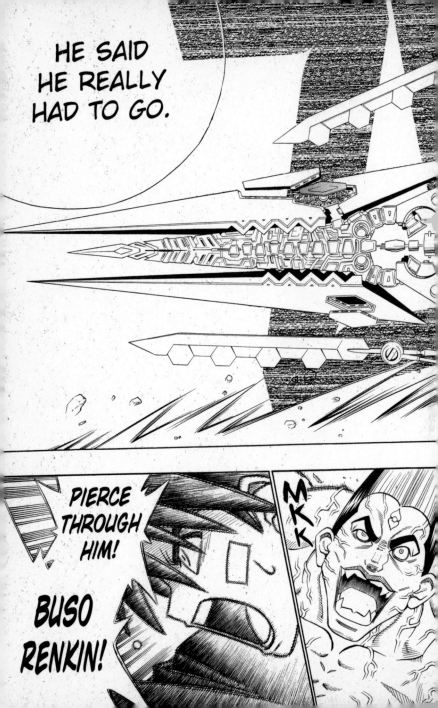

YUP.

KAZUKI MUTO. THIS BOY HAS THE QUALITIES OF BECOMING A TRUE WARRIOR!

I'M SURE YOU'RE NOT GOING TO LISTEN TO ME EVEN IF I TELL YOU NO.

I DON'T WANT YOU DYING IN FRONT OF ME AGAIN!

FINE THEN! I'LL WORK YOU TO THE BONE AS MY WARRIOR APPRENTICE!

DO YOU SWEAR TO ALWAYS FOLLOW MY ORDERS! WELL?

SALUTE!

ROGER!

SO...

NOW WHAT?

I KNEW IT.

...SORRY. I FORGOT TO TELL YOU.

WHAT'S YOUR NAME?

LISTEN. MY NAME IS...

- King Cobra-type Homunculus
- He used to be a professor at Ginsei Academy. Being an educator was just a job for him and he didn't show any interest in the students. He was the homeroom professor of Papillon Mask, the Homunculi creator. He was turned into a Homunculus for saying, "You should just drop out of school" to Papillon Mask.
- He turned out to be a relatively well balanced Homunculus. After turning into a Homunculus he was able to continue teaching and his social skills improved.

Author's Notes
- Mahiro needed to get eaten by him and get saved. In order to get past this event, I chose a snake that swallows their prey whole.
- I chose to make him into a cold, unsociable character because it took too many pages to build up the characters surrounding Kazuki. He turned out to be more snakelike so it all worked out in the end.

No. 2 Homunculus Mita

Character File

No. 3 Homunculus Saruwatari and his minions

- A group of mountain gorilla, monkey, baboon, chimp-type Homunculi.
- They used to be Yakuza gang members. Saruwatari's minions were all his yakuza underlings and friends when he used to be in a motorcycle gang. They were turned into Homunculi for trying to mug Papillon Mask one night in town.
- They turned out to be average quality Homunculi. Being monkeys, they strictly follow a social hierarchy based on strength. They are easy to command and manage. The reason why there are so many of them is because they were also research subjects for '???' type Homunculus.

Author's Notes
- Due to the page limitations I created a simple-minded, easy to understand character, a powerhouse gorilla. He also needed underlings so I made them into a pack of monkeys.

CHAPTER 3
HOMUNCULUS'S IDENTITY

TSU
MU
RA

TO
KI
KO

AIEEE!

OKAKURA! YOU PERVERT!

THERE'S A GIRL'S PHONE NUMBER IN IT?

AIEEE!

KAZUKI'S CELLPHONE

...

NOOOO!

THAT'S WHAT YOU GET FOR LOOKING IN SOMEONE'S CELLPHONE.

OKAKURA'S A PERVERT?

RUSTLE RUSTLE

YOU'RE A PERVERT?

OKAKURA, THE PERVERT!

I'M STILL TIRED BUT IT'S OKAY.

YEAH, I'LL BE FINE.

YEAH.

OH. HI TOKIKO.

DAMN IT! LOOK AT HIM HAVING SWEET STRAWBERRY TALKS!

WHAT ARE THEY TALKING ABOUT?

...BERRY.

STRAW...

APPARENTLY SHE'S NOT AN IMAGINARY GIRLFRIEND.

I READ HIS LIPS.

WHAT?! WHO ARE YOU REALLY?

YOU CAN HEAR THEM?

NO.

THEY'RE GOING TO MEET UP AFTER SCHOOL AT THE GHOST FACTORY.

94

GLOP BLOOP

SHW

...A MORE FRIENDLY APPROACH.

NO, LET'S TRY...

IT'S SAFE TO ASSUME IT'S SOMEONE WHO HAS SOME TYPE OF LINK TO ALCHEMY THAT LIVES IN THIS AREA...

WE CAN GUESS THEIR INTENTIONS BUT THERE'S NOTHING CONCLUSIVE AT THIS POINT TO DETERMINE ANYTHING.

...FOR HIS RESEARCH.

HE'LL DO ANYTHING AT ANY COST...

THE CREATOR THINKS NOTHING OF HUMAN LIFE.

THE ONLY THING WE KNOW FOR SURE IS...

96

YEAH. I WASN'T EXPECTING HER TO ATTACK US IN THE AIR, TANGLED IN THE CLOTH.

ARE YOU ALL RIGHT MASTER?

SHOOM

AND THE OTHER GUY WITH THE LANCE!

I MUSTN'T UNDERESTIMATE THE GIRL WITH THE EXECUTION SCYTHE.

VHH

TOKI-KO!

ARE YOU ALL RIGHT TOKIKO?

FwwwW

IT'S THE SAME AS KAZUKI'S!

I GOT A CLUE.

HIS SCHOOL UNIFORM.

SHAKE SHAKE

CHINK

ARE YOU ALL RIGHT?

YEAH.

KSH
KSH
KCHINK
KRSHR

IF WE INCLUDE THE CORE THAT I DESTROYED EARLIER...

WE DESTROYED 16 HOMUNCULI LAST NIGHT.

PI

THERE WERE 20 INCUBATORS IN THE BASEMENT.

THE PAPILLON MASK CREATOR.

THREE ENEMY HOMUNCULI REMAIN AND...

...

THE REMAINING THREE ARE PROBABLY THE CREATOR'S BODYGUARDS.

THEY'RE GOING TO BE POWERFUL.

WE WON'T LOSE.

THAT'S RIGHT. THE BUSO RENKIN WERE CREATED TO ANNIHILATE THEM.

WE HAVE TO WIN!

YEAH BUT...

THEY WILL BE DESTROYED!

Tokiko Tsumura

- Bust 78, Waist 55, Hip 79
- Born: August 7th; Leo; Blood type: A; 17 years old.
- Favorites: Rice balls, purple, airy spaces
- Dislikes: Homunculi, unnecessary deaths
- Hobby: Training
- Things she is good at: Getting dressed fast (From uniform to gym clothes in a flash!)
- Affiliation: Organization that governs the Alchemist Warriors (Name has not been revealed at this point)

Author's Notes

- She represents the Warrior Heroine I've been wanting to draw for the last four years. I have been continuously conceptualizing her.
- As she is the one guiding Kazuki I've added a sisterly quality to her. (I imagine her to be like an after-school club president that is looking after the younger members)
- I kept thinking how easy she is to draw but after taking a closer look she looks like Battousai from Rurouni Kenshin...
- The scar on her nose is Kurosaki Sensei's idea. We were just talking about random things and it came up while we were talking about "What would you do if you were to draw a female pro wrestling story?" With his consent I borrowed his idea.
- I borrowed her last name Tsumura from a character named Sayoko Tsumura from Riku Anda's novel, "The Sixth Sayoko" (*Rokuban me no Sayoko*). Sayoko's mysteriousness is somewhat reflected in Tokiko's character. I came up with the kanji combination for the name "Tokiko".
- I was hoping she'd be a Warrior Heroine that equals the male character's presence but currently he's by far the most popular character in Buso Renkin... You can do it, Kazuki!

KAZUKI.

WHAT IS IT TOKIKO?

CHAPTER 4: PARASITIC HOMUNCULUS

BUT IT'S NOT ENOUGH TO JUST SAY YOU WON'T LET MORE PEOPLE DIE.

YOU'VE MADE YOUR DECISION.

YOU'VE BEEN GIVEN A POWER.

YEAH.

YEAH.

IF YOU ARE DETERMINED TO SAVE LIVES ...

YOU NEED TO MASTER YOUR BUSO RENKIN!

HEY BROTHER!

THERE THEY ARE!

CHAPTER 4:
PARASITIC HOMUNCULUS

AAAAAAA!! WHAT ARE YOU DOING HERE?

FINE. I'LL BE POLITE AND I'LL EXCUSE MYSELF.

I DIDN'T TELL THEM ANYTHING.

YOU TOLD THEM YOU WERE COMING HERE?

MY BROTHER HAS A GIRL-FRIEND!

!

YOU'RE RIGHT!

EHHH?

WHEN DID THIS HAPPEN? WHEN DID THIS HAPPEN?

CON-GRATS!

TAKE US OUT.

KAAAZUKIIII!

HUH?

EEEEH?

GIRL-FRIEND?

111

117

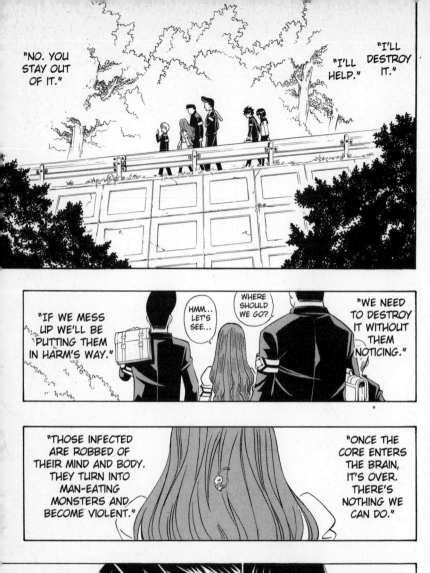

THE SUN SET A LONG TIME AGO.

YOU'RE FINALLY AWAKE.

I'M FINE. THANKS TO YOU.

I'M FINE.

THROB THROB THROB THROB

LOTS OF BRUISES...

...ON YOU, I MEAN.

JOLT

ANY INJURIES?

IT'S OKAY.

...WHAT ABOUT THE HOMUNCULUS?

YOU PROTECTED ME, SO...

IT DIDN'T MANAGE TO ENTER MY BRAIN.

GLARE

WHY ARE YOU APOLO-GIZING?

YOU DID ABSOLUTELY NOTHING WRONG.

I'M SORRY ...

SQUEEZE

I'M STILL SORRY THOUGH.

THAT GOES FOR YOU AS WELL.

IMAGINE THE IRREPARABLE DAMAGE IF YOUR SISTER OR ONE OF YOUR FRIENDS GOT INFECTED.

DON'T APOLO-GIZE.

ON THE CONTRARY, YOU DID GREAT.

...IS SOMETHING I'M NOT WILLING TO DO.

PUTTING YOUR LIFE IN DANGER AGAIN...

SW

Mahiro Muto

- Height: 161 cm; Weight: 49kg
- Bust 85, Waist 59, Hip 88
- Born: February 29th; Pisces; Blood type: O; 15 years old
- Favorites: Mentaiko spaghetti, earth tones, Chi-chin, Sa-chan & Tokiko, reading manga
- Dislikes: Green veggie juice, marathons
- Hobbies: Checking out new candy products
- Things she is good at: Being outgoing (she can have a friendly chit-chat with someone who she's known for five minutes!)
- Affiliation: Private Ginsei Academy First Year High School Student Classroom A, Dorm Resident

Author's Notes

- She was the character with the most revisions. She was first cast as an older classmate, the "Heroine who got left behind a year." She was a very challenging character to manipulate. (Certain things haven't changed, like her appearance. She doesn't look like she is Kazuki's younger sister…) I planned her to be the Heroine representing normalcy, opposite of Tokiko, but I couldn't mesh it well together. Instead I decided to make her relationship with Kazuki simpler! She is in order, a classmate, a girl who he grew up with together, a cousin, an older sister, and lastly, a younger sister.
- Her uniform is a typical sailor uniform but my friend advised me I should play with it a little. I used a Gothic Lolita Magazine as reference and designed it. Now looking at it, I think I might have had too much fun with the design?
- She was supposed to complement a side of Kazuki's daily life and be a well-balanced character that would feed off of Kazuki's jokes but as the chapters went on… Never underestimate the Muto family genetics.

CHAPTER 5:
VS. KAWAZUI (Part 1)

ARE YOU STILL NOT SLEEPING WELL?

YAWN
...

YOU NEED TO GET A FULL NIGHT'S REST.

DON'T WORRY. I'LL THINK OF A NAME FOR YOUR LANCE.

NO. THAT'S NOT THE REASON.

I'M TELLING YOU THIS NOW BUT IT'S REALLY A DRASTIC MEASURE TO USE THE KAKUGANE AS A HEART REPLACEMENT.

THAT'S WHY YOU SHOULDN'T PUSH YOURSELF TOO HARD.

IF YOU FEEL ANY PAIN OR IF YOU'RE NOT FEELING WELL TELL ME. DON'T HIDE IT.

IT IS?

ARE YOU OKAY, TOKIKO?

...

YOU'VE BEEN HOLDING YOUR STOMACH SINCE LAST NIGHT...

CAPTURE THE PAPILLON MASK CREATOR!

I NEED TO MASTER HOW TO USE THIS LANCE IN A WEEK AND...

TOKIKO SAID I SHOULD GET A LOT OF REST BUT ...

I HAVE TO WORK HARD!

POSE

I'LL DO A THOUSAND SWINGS LIKE I DID LAST NIGHT.

TWO.

VSH

VSH

ONE.

I'M NOT SURE WHAT I'M SUPPOSED TO DO EXACTLY SO...

I'LL APPLY THE BASICS FROM THE LEARN-AT-HOME KARATE TECHNIQUES.

VSH

THREE.

DAY TWO

MASTER!

COUGH.

COUGH.

COUGH.

RIDING ON YOUR BACK, NOT THINKING ABOUT MY CONDITION.

HAH HAH... I GUESS THIS IS WHAT I GET FOR...

SHAKE SHAKE

ARE YOU ALL RIGHT?

...

I DON'T, SORRY...

THE MINI-FROGS HAVE TERRIBLE EYESIGHT.

YES?

BY THE WAY, KAWAZUI.

YOU REALLY DON'T KNOW WHO THE OTHER MALE WARRIOR IS?

WE KNOW THEIR EVERY MOVE THROUGH KAWAZUI AND THE MINI-FROGS ...

THERE IS NO NEED TO TAKE FURTHER ACTION. IF I TAKE THREE MORE DAYS OFF FROM SCHOOL THAT FEMALE WARRIOR IS FINISHED.

138

142

146

· A Surinam Toad Homunculus.
· He used to be the Creator's online buddy and a fellow recluse. They got [...]
  but they got in an argument stemming from something small. He sent ha[...]
  the Creator so he turned him into a Homunculus.
· An inferior-quality Homunculus. It has useful abilities such as creating m[...]
  making them do his bidding but Kawazui himself is rather questionable.

Author's Notes

· The story required a sneaky character who spies on people so after putt[...]
  thought into it I decided to use a Surinam Toad.
· To my surprise Kawazui turned out to have a lot of character. I enjoyed [...]
  character a lot. I felt like I had a small revelation about the future Creato[...]
  while drawing Kawazui.

No. 6 Homunculus Kawazui

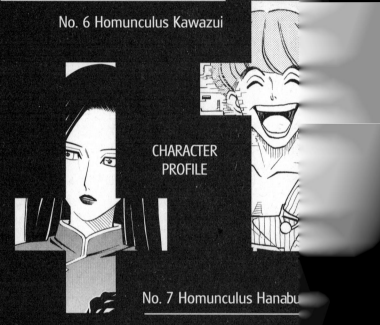

CHARACTER
PROFILE

No. 7 Homunculus Hanabu[...]

· A rose Homunculus.
· She was a tutor the Creator's father hired for him. She tried seducing the[...]
  his family fortune but the Creator saw through her and turned her into a [...]
· She was the first Homunculus the Papillon Mask created. Using Hanafu[...]
  Creator collected samples from the zoo for his latter Homunculus creatio[...]

Author's Notes

· I made her into a rose in order to use a plant's ability to expand and gr[...]
  idea to cover the dorm with vines but that idea got cut due to the storyli[...]
· Due to the tight schedule I had to design her impromptu. I wish I could [...]
  her sexier with wavy hair.

BUSO RENKIN!

FLASH

CALLING OUT YOUR WEAPON, EH? I'LL DO IT TOO.

TRANS-FORM!

PKK

PKK

PKK

HOMUN-CULUS ...

CHAPTER 6: VS. KAWAZUI (PART 2)

TRAINING ROUTINE!!

Run 5km

Swing 1000 times

Simulate a battle in your mind ♡

SECRET

A TRAINING ROUTINE!

...NOW IT MAKES SENSE. THIS IS THE REASON HE'S NOT GETTING ENOUGH SLEEP THIS TIME.

HE'S NOT HERE...

HUH?

CLIK

THAT'S SO CUTE ...

I GOT SOME GOOD STUFF! IT'S YOUR FAVORITE NUDIE MAGS ...

HEY KAZUKI! YOU HERE?

HEH HEH ♡

CREAK

BUT HE DOESN'T UNDERSTAND... HE'S NOT GOING TO BE ABLE TO MASTER THE BUSO RENKIN WITH THIS METHOD...

156

TOKI-KO?!

...SAY WHAT!

HUH?

TOKIKO. WHAT ARE YOU DOING HERE?

HEY.

Aaaa... I'm no longer a pervert!

ANYWAY, YOU NEED TO CONTROL YOUR PASSIONS.

I SEE. SO KAZUKI IS INTO THIS TYPE OF STUFF.

TOKI-KO?

!

HE HASN'T COME HOME TODAY. HE WASN'T AT DINNER EITHER. THOUGH.

DO YOU KNOW WHERE KAZUKI IS?

NO. HE'S BEEN SKIPPING OUT THE LAST TWO, THREE DAYS AFTER DINNER.

TOSS

NOW I HAVE A VALID EXCUSE FOR MASTER.

ZA

ZA

ZA

HUH? HOW DO YOU TURN THIS BACK INTO A KAKUGANE?

TWITCH

HUH? I'M STILL ALIVE...

THAT'S WHY I'M OKAY EVEN IF I HAVE A HOLE THROUGH MY CHEST.

OH... THAT'S RIGHT. MY CHEST IS EMPTY RIGHT NOW.

HEH HEH.

GOT ME A PRIZE!

PSH PSH

?!!

THE MINI-FROGS WERE... ANNIHILATED...

EACH BUSO RENKIN HAS A "FEATURE" THAT CAN'T BE MIMICKED BY MODERN SCIENCE!

I GOT IT!

TOKIKO'S VALKYRIE SKIRT HAS FOUR ROBOT ARMS THAT MOVE SWIFTLY AND ACCURATELY.

Chapter 1: New Life

· The series began with the concept of "Incredible and strange beings battling it out" but then I realized, it was a "Romantic Comedy Wannabe"…. I was full of anxieties.

· I tried changing the art style a bit so you can tell where I was drawing with great agony in several sections. The artwork juuuust isn't right. Mahiro looks completely different now compared to the beginning…

· I created the page flow right around when I bought a cellphone so I ended up using the cellphone a lot. I was thinking how useful it was at first but I realized it was too useful. I ended up stressing over how to use it in several places…

· This is a commonly used structural format. Maybe that's why people would ask where I got the idea from, or point out that I copied it from XYZ in their letters. I got it from Ultraman. (I'm an old man so I know very little about the anime and videogames that are out now…) My first editor figured it out right away.

Chapter 2: Midnight Run

· I wanted to state that the Alchemy in my manga is different from Alchemy in the traditional sense so I ended up squishing my explanation in there. Unfortunately, I don't think a lot of people know what Alchemy really is.

· Kazuki's attack from this chapter is my favorite scene in the whole volume.

· The reason why I didn't reveal Tokiko's name in the first two chapters is because I didn't have the opportunity. It was a complete structural blunder.

· I got the title from one of my favorite movies.

Chapter 3: Homunculus's Identity

· This chapter continued to set the stage. I know making the setting too complicated equates to a boring manga but… I paid very close attention.

· In the introduction of the Papillon Mask Creator, my editor at the time was like, "I'm not sure about this mask…" It was an obvious critique but I ended up agonizing over it. With my friends and assistants' encouragement I decided to go with it. At this point, I had no idea things would turn out like that later…

· This is the chapter I started to feel like I grasped Kazuki's "space cadet" character.

Chapter 4: Parasitic Homunculus

· In order to create a "time limit" and "suppress Tokiko's power for the time being" she becomes ill from the parasitic Homunculus.

· I tried a touch of "Passion" by showing Tokiko's stomach a little bit! I was so embarrassed I drew it while my assistants were asleep. Thoughts such as "I wonder if they'll say something?" and "Will they make a comment?" were racing through my head while I nervously handed them the pages but no response. The pink typhoon ended up passing through only my head.

· The scene where Kazuki is protecting Tokiko from the boulder was an idea that came up suddenly when I was creating the page flow. I think the only person who would do something like this instinctively is Kazuki. It's a side of him that I'd really like to expand.

CHAPTER 7:
YOU'RE A LITTLE STRONGER

DYING REALLY HURTS...

BUSO RENKIN!

DO NOT UNDERESTIMATE AN ALCHEMIST WARRIOR, MONSTER!

PAMIII?!

IEEEN

DRIP

...SO FILTHY.

I'LL DESTROY AS MANY HOMUNCULI AS I CAN BEFORE I BECOME A MONSTER!

IF I BECOME A HOMUNCULUS THE FIRST THING I'LL DO IS GO AFTER THE PAPILLON MASK CREATOR!

182

NEW LIFE (THE END)

Chapter 5: VS. Kawazui (Part 1)

· The theme to this chapter was for Kazuki to fight on his own. It took an entire chapter to make him stern, as he's been so happy-go-lucky. It made me worry a little about what's yet to come.

· Personally I liked the uniform and phys-ed clothes joke. I liked it so much I brought it up again later.

· Kawazui's overalls got both positive & negative reviews as per its creepiness.

Chapter 6: VS. Kawazui (Part 2)

· This chapter's theme is a continuation of Kazuki fighting alone. I started drawing without finalizing parts of the page flow. I was really stressing about how to make a normal boy's mindset shift into a life of battles. To be honest I'm still stressing out about it. I felt like I finally figured out the reason why fantasy manga that has both battles and normal everyday life themes are sweeping the Shonen Manga industry. But my last two manga were similar to that as well. I'll do better next time…

· I heard comments about how the battle scenes didn't feel like it was enough because it only lasted for one chapter. I didn't feel like I got everything out either. I'll do better next time…

· The comment in chapter 4, "You need to control your passions," was a comment I was also making to myself.

Chapter 7: You're a Little Stronger

· I had to follow a bunch of restrictions for this chapter. Some made me cry and some made me laugh.

· The Kawazui mini-frogs were originally just the head and the spine. I designed them with machine-like parts, but that idea got shot down as it resembled a head too much. I ended up adding the body, but for some reason it started to get an eerie look to it, and I was very satisfied with it at the end. It was pure dumb luck.

· I imagined Hanabusa to be a character that puts emphasis on "Beauty". I wanted her to make a comment towards Tokiko's scar and have Tokiko reply so the plot would focus on her scar a little. I received a critique how it would be insensitive to say the scar on her face was ugly as people actually do have scars and injuries on their face from accidents and illnesses so I opted not to. I was a little disappointed but I totally understood why I shouldn't.

· The idea to directly show Tokiko shoving her fingers in Hanabusa's eyes did not pass as some children might actually act on it. Instead we hid it using the word bubble. This attack is where I could clearly show Tokiko's ruthlessness and I had envisioned it before I started the series. When the idea did not go though I was rather disappointed.

· Shonen Manga have a lot of restrictions you have to follow, which is a pain, but by working within those restrictions you learn new ways to express something. I think this is a good way to learn. As long as I get to grow I'm totally fine.

Hence… →

To be continued.

武装錬金
BUSO RENKIN

Coming Next Volume

Kazuki and Tokiko scramble to uncover the identity of the homunculus creator. Desperate to find the antidote to the homunculus that has attached itself to Tokiko, Kazuki suspects a sickly student at his school as the perpetrator. With time running out before the homunculus reaches Tokiko's brain and kills her, Tokiko hands her kakugane—an alchemical device that transforms into a buso renkin—to Kazuki. Let's just hope it's not too late...

Available in October 2006!

BOBOBO-BO BO-BOBO™

ONLY $7.99

On Sale Now!

BO-BOBO SAYS NO NO NO TO THOSE WHO WOULD HUNT HAIR!

BOBOBO-BO BO-BOBO
Story and Art by Yoshio Sawai

FREE PREVIEW ISSUE!
of SHONEN JUMP Magazine!

THE WORLD'S MOST POPULAR MANGA

www.shonenjump.com

SHONEN JUMP Magazine: Contains Yu-Gi-Oh!, One Piece, Naruto, Shaman King, YuYu Hakusho and other HOT manga—STORIES NEVER SEEN IN THE ANIME!
Plus, get the latest on what's happening in trading cards, video games, toys and more!

Check out this ultra cool magazine for FREE! Then when you decide you must have SHONEN JUMP every month we will send you 11 more issues (12 in all) for only $29.95. A Price so low it's like getting 6 issues FREE!

But that's not all: You'll also become a member of the 𝒮𝒥 Sub Club with your paid subscription!

Get your FREE Preview Issue!

SHONEN JUMP Magazine — the blockbuster English-language version of Japan's #1 action comic book every month features 300+ pages of the hottest manga titles available in the U.S. Plus the latest on what's happening in cards, video games, toys and more!

YES! Send me my FREE preview issue of **SHONEN JUMP** Magazine. If I like it I will enjoy 11 more issues (12 in all) for ONLY **$29.95**. That's 50% OFF the cover price!

50% OFF the cover price!

NAME

ADDRESS

CITY   STATE   ZIP

E-MAIL ADDRESS

☐ MY CHECK IS ENCLOSED   ☐ BILL ME LATER

Make checks payable to: SHONEN JUMP. Canada add US $12. No foreign orders.
Credit card payments made SECURE & EASY at www.SHONENJUMP.com

Allow 6-8 weeks for delivery.

THE WORLD'S MOST POPULAR MANGA
www.shonenjump.com

𝒮𝒥 SUB CLUB Benefits!

Access to exclusive Sub Club only areas of www.SHONENJUMP.com

Your Issues Delivered First

Cool Gifts Included With Some Issues

YU-GI-OH! © 1996 by KAZUKI TAKAHASHI / SHUEISHA Inc.

P6SGN1

Check us out on the web!

www.shonenjump.com

SHONEN JUMP
THE WORLD'S MOST POPULAR MANGA

COMPLETE OUR SURVEY AND LET US KNOW WHAT YOU THINK!

Name: _____

Address: _____

City: _____ **State:** _____ **Zip:** _____

E-mail: _____

☐ Male ☐ Female **Date of Birth** (mm/dd/yyyy): ___ / ___ / _____ (Under 13? Parental consent required.)

❶ Do you purchase SHONEN JUMP magazine?

☐ Yes ☐ No

If **YES**, do you subscribe?

☐ Yes ☐ No

If **NO**, how often do you purchase SHONEN JUMP magazine?

☐ 1-3 issues a year ☐ 4-6 issues a year ☐ more than 7 issues a year

❷ Which SHONEN JUMP Volume 1 manga did you purchase this time? _____

Will you purchase subsequent volumes?

☐ Yes ☐ No

❸ How did you learn about this title? (check all that apply)

☐ Favorite title ☐ Advertisement ☐ Article
☐ Gift ☐ Recommendation ☐ Special offer
☐ Through TV animation ☐ Read excerpt in SHONEN JUMP magazine
☐ Website ☐ Other _____

❹ Of the titles that are serialized in SHONEN JUMP magazine, have you purchased the paperback manga volumes?

☐ Yes ☐ No

If **YES**, which ones have you purchased? (check all that apply)

☐ Hikaru no Go ☐ Naruto ☐ One Piece ☐ Shaman King
☐ Yu-Gi-Oh!: Millennium World ☐ YuYu Hakusho

If **YES**, what were your reasons for purchasing? (please pick up to 3)

- [ ] A favorite title
- [ ] A favorite creator/artist
- [ ] I like the smaller size
- [ ] There are extras that aren't in the magazine
- [ ] I want to read it in one go
- [ ] The quality of printing is better than the magazine
- [ ] I want to read it over and over again
- [ ] Recommendation
- [ ] Special offer
- [ ] Other

If **NO**, why did/would you not purchase it?

- [ ] I'm happy just reading it in the magazine
- [ ] It's not worth buying the manga volume
- [ ] All the manga pages are in black and white, unlike the magazine
- [ ] There are other manga volumes that I prefer
- [ ] There are too many to collect for each title
- [ ] It's too small
- [ ] Other _____

5 Of the titles NOT serialized in the magazine, which ones have you purchased? (check all that apply)

- [ ] Beet the Vandel Buster
- [ ] Black Cat
- [ ] Bleach
- [ ] Bobobo-bo Bo-bobo
- [ ] Claymore
- [ ] D.Gray-man
- [ ] Death Note
- [ ] Dragon Ball
- [ ] Dragon Ball Z
- [ ] Dr. Slump
- [ ] Eyeshield 21
- [ ] Hunter x Hunter
- [ ] I"s
- [ ] JoJo's Bizarre Adventure
- [ ] Knights of the Zodiac
- [ ] Legendz
- [ ] The Prince of Tennis
- [ ] Rurouni Kenshin
- [ ] Ultimate Muscle
- [ ] Whistle!
- [ ] Yu-Gi-Oh!
- [ ] Yu-Gi-Oh!: Duelist
- [ ] None
- [ ] Other

If you did purchase any of the above, what were your reasons for purchasing?

- [ ] A favorite title
- [ ] A favorite creator/artist
- [ ] Read a preview in SHONEN JUMP magazine and wanted to read the rest of the story
- [ ] Recommendation
- [ ] Other

Will you purchase subsequent volumes if available?

- [ ] Yes
- [ ] No

6 Of the following, what manga-related books would you like to buy? (check all that apply)

- [ ] Art books
- [ ] Character profile books
- [ ] Novels/Novelizations
- [ ] None of these

7 What race/ethnicity do you consider yourself? (please check one)

- [ ] Asian/Pacific Islander
- [ ] Black/African American
- [ ] Hispanic/Latino
- [ ] Native American/Alaskan Native
- [ ] White/Caucasian
- [ ] Other

THANK YOU! Please send the completed form to:

VIZ Media Survey
42 Catharine St.
Poughkeepsie, NY 12601

VIZ media